D1609012

ARTHUR MARX'S
GROUCHO
A PHOTOGRAPHIC JOURNEY

EDITOR
Frank Ferrante

DESIGNER
Jerry Eggers

PHOTO EDITOR
Ralph Torres

With Comments & Photography by
ARTHUR MARX

Published in 2001 by Phoenix Marketing Services, Inc.
2809 Pomona Boulevard
Pomona, CA 97168

Library of Congress Catalog Number: 00-111645
ISBN: 0-9707143-0-0

Printed in the United States of America by Phoenix Marketing Services

FOR LOIS
LOVE, ARTHUR

FOR AMANDA
LOVE, FRANK

FOREWORD

"GROUCHO'S GREAT!" I blurted from the top of the metal stairs outside the renown Ambassador Hotel in Los Angeles.

At a 1976 Ambassador Hotel appearance, Groucho waves to Frank Ferrante.

My eighty-five year-old hero slowly gazed up from the drive below and tentatively waved. It was 1976, but I still cringe a bit at the rawness of that impulse to shout out my allegiance. But, how else could I express my gratitude, my thanks for his exhilarating irreverence, his contempt for all things conventional, his wild unpredictability? He couldn't shuffle off without my letting him and the world know that I loved him. I was his student. And, nightly, I prayed that some day I would make people laugh the way Groucho Marx did. My prayer was answered...literally. Ten years later to the week, I opened in New York portraying my childhood alter ego at age eighty-five in "Groucho: A Life in Revue."

The play was written by Groucho's son, Arthur Marx, and our collaboration as work mates and friends began in 1985 when Arthur discovered me performing as his father at the University of Southern California. I was twenty-two years old.

For the past fifteen years, I have been privy to much of the lore and truths swirling around the legendary Marx Family. Without a doubt, the most meaningful outgrowth of this childhood obsession is my dear friendship with Arthur and his wife, Lois. In fact, the concept of this book ignited over their kitchen table during one of Lois' many glorious lunches. One afternoon at their Bel Air home, I was finishing my third helping as their Yorkshire terrier, Lily, nipped at my shoes under the table.

I paged through Arthur's scrapbooks riveted by his candid, one of a kind photographs – photos of Hollywood and Beverly Hills in the 1930's, the Marx Brothers at work at MGM and unusually intimate family shots. Arthur's composition was captivating and use of lighting effective. His color photography of sunsets and landscapes was equally evocative. I said, "Arthur, there's a book here."

Soon after that lunch, Arthur handed me a small, flat, oak box. In the box were dozens of canisters containing developed film rolls – mostly negatives that had never been printed. We carefully went through every roll and discovered gem after gem. As a result, the core of this book consists primarily of Arthur Marx's photography from the 1930's to the present. More than half of this published collection is either photographs taken by Arthur or borrowed from his personal collection. Most have never before been seen.

To flesh out the Marx Family time-line in pictures, we turned to Marx Brothers archivist and expert, Paul Wesolowski. Paul has kindly contributed many rare and previously unseen photos to complement Arthur's story. Some photos that have been previously published are showcased here at their best advantage. My hope is that the uninitiated will be taken in by the subject matter and die hard fans will rejoice at this new contribution.

Frank Ferrante, Editor
October 2, 2000
Los Angeles, California

Frank Ferrante at the age of eleven performing as Groucho in 1974.

INTRODUCTION

When I was twelve years old, and understandably not sure how I wanted to make a living when I grew up, my father, Groucho Marx, warned me, "You can do anything you want – just as long as you don't become an actor. It's a lousy life."

By the term "lousy," he was referring to the hard times he and his brothers had to go through when they were climbing up the show business ladder. They began in small time vaudeville as teen-agers when pay was little, bookings were sparse and theater owners tyrants – and continued their way to Broadway in a revue called "I'll Say She Is"– a success they didn't achieve until they were in their mid-thirties.

I had no interest in becoming an actor – especially after my one attempt at acting in a grammar school production of "Little Women." I played the part of Professor Baer with an atrocious German accent. My German dialect was so bad, in fact, that when I opened my mouth for the first time on the stage to declaim what was allegedly a straight line, my father roared with laughter and my Uncle Harpo, who was also in the audience, fell in the aisle in hysterics.

Perhaps, it was that performance, and not the vaudeville hardships my father claimed to have undergone on his way to Broadway, that caused him to warn me not to become an actor. It certainly convinced me.

A portrait I took of my best friend, Michael Levee, Jr., in the 1930's.

In 1934, my best friend, Michael Levee, Jr., the son of a successful Hollywood agent, had just been given one of the first 35 mm cameras, a Leica, for a birthday present, which caused him to venture into the world of candid photography. The pictures he took excited me, so I asked my father for a camera thinking perhaps I could make a living taking pictures.

Unfortunately, Leica's cost a couple hundred, even in those days, which was more than my father wanted to spend. So, he compromised and bought me a $12 Argus. It had an F 4.5 lens, a shutter speed of 200 and it used 35 millimeter film. "It looks like a Leica," my father pointed out. "So, who'll know the difference?"

At home, in our house in Beverly Hills, my father allowed me to convert a pantry we had on the second floor into a darkroom. Moreover, as much as he hated posing for studio or newspaper photographers, he never objected to my taking candid photos of him doing just about anything. When I wasn't in school or playing in tennis tournaments, he took me to MGM Studios in Culver City, where he was under contract, and encouraged me to hang around the set and shoot candid photos of him, his brothers and the other actors in action.

I never became a professional photographer, although I've used many of my photographs to illustrate magazine articles I've written for all the major publications. But photography has been a wonderful hobby, and I'm still taking pictures today. And wonder of all wonders, I've kept most of the negatives from my camera work dating back to when I had my first Argus. If I hadn't, this book wouldn't exist to illustrate the story of Groucho, the Marx Brothers and my family in Hollywood. My family was there for Hollywood's growth from a one horse town to the thriving, smog-filled, traffic congested movie capital of the world it is today.

Arthur Marx
October 2, 2000
Bel Air, California

Arthur Marx at fourteen in 1935 with one of his first cameras.

My father Julius Henry Marx (left) a.k.a. Groucho in 1905 at fifteen about to embark on a seventy-two year theatrical career beginning as one third of the singing Leroy Trio. Here he is with a full head of curly, black hair, a celluloid collar, a carnation in his button hole and a smile – actually the beginning of a sneer – on his face that fans would always associate with him.

Julius "Groucho" Marx at seventeen (right). Before he became successful in show business, Groucho smoked nickel cigars. Only once did he spring for a ten cent stogie, and that was the result of an ad he'd seen in a cigar store window. The ad promised the smoker of the La Preferencia "Thirty Glorious Minutes in Havana." Since Groucho figured he'd never get to Havana any other way, he sprung for it. But it only took twenty minutes to smoke the cigar. So, Groucho confronted the store owner and demanded a new cigar. The owner gave him one, but with the same results. Again, he confronted the owner and, again, he was given a fresh cigar. But, the third one burned no longer than the other two. Feeling he'd been victimized, Groucho brought back what was left of the third stogie to the store owner and asked him what he planned to do about it. The owner's reply was to boot the young upstart out on the sidewalk with the threat of calling police if he didn't get lost. "You couldn't believe the advertising in those days anymore than you can today," my father told me after relating the above story.

Groucho's mother, my grandmother, the indomitable Minnie Schoenberg at age seventeen. All the Marx Brothers credited their ambitious stage struck mother for their success. She drove them. She made them. And she lived to see her boys become Broadway stars. She died at sixty-five in 1929.

A portrait of Groucho's father, Sam "Frenchy" Marx, who was a tailor. In fact, he could have inspired the tune "Sam, You Made the Pants Too Long." As Father put it, he was a "lousy tailor" but "a gentle man."

The Marx Brothers' Uncle Al Shean (formerly Schoenberg) of the legendary vaudeville comedy team of Gallagher & Shean was responsible for writing the Marx Brothers' early vaudeville efforts.

Ed Mack 1896

Here he is in 1896 on the Orpheum Circuit pictured as a member of the Manhattan Comedy Four prior to his partnering with Eddie Gallagher. Al is second from the right.

In 1917, after the United States entered the first World War, Harpo, Gummo, Zeppo, Groucho and Chico (not pictured) bought a farm near La Grange, Illinois, where they planned on raising chickens for eggs in order to help Uncle Sam combat wartime food shortages. They figured that being in a business like farming would keep them out of the Army. The brothers were city boys, however, and knew nothing about raising chickens and selling eggs for the commercial markets. For some reason, they couldn't get their chickens to lay eggs, which would endanger their draft deferments. So, on the morning inspectors were due, fast thinking Groucho and Chico drove into La Grange where they bought twelve dozen boxes of eggs at the grocery store. They then brought them back to the farm, and put the eggs under the hens in the chicken coop – a caper they might have pulled off if the eggs they had purchased hadn't been white eggs. Unfortunately, their hens were Long Island Reds, which only laid brown eggs. Luckily for the world of comedy, none of the Marx Brothers got drafted because Groucho and Chico were deferred for bad eyesight, Zeppo was too young, and no one knows why the Army didn't want Harpo – probably because he wouldn't talk.

Me and Julius H. Marx, as Groucho was known in 1924, are sitting on kiddy cars in front of the Marx family home in Richmond Hill, Long Island in the photo on the left. When I say the Marx family, I mean that the home contained all the Marx Brothers and their wives and children, and the Marx Brothers' mother and father, Sam and Minnie Marx. We were living under one roof prior to the opening on Broadway of "I'll Say She Is," the Brothers' first big hit. Note thirty-three year-old Groucho's real hair mustache.

And, here I am on the right at the age of three, standing in the front yard of the Marx family home. My mother had my head shaved because she was told it would grow back thicker. It still hasn't.

During the days of big-time vaudeville, it was the custom for each act on the bill to have a baseball team. Groucho's position was catcher on the "Home Again" team, and a mighty fine catcher he was, as you can see by the photo below. Will Rogers, who was a few years older than the Marx clan, was on the bill with the Marx Brothers in "Home Again." They were all great friends, except when the Marx team was playing Will Rogers' team, on which the rope-twirling monologist's position was second base.

One afternoon, Groucho hit a single, but tried to stretch it into a double. Rogers was about fifteen feet off the bag when he caught the ball and called Groucho, who had just reached second base, "Out." Groucho protested the call, pointing out to Rogers that he had to have his foot on second base in order for it to be a forced out. Rogers looked at Groucho, and with a straight face, said, "Listen, Groucho, when you get to be my age, anyplace you stand is second base."

That's my mother, Ruth, and I on the right, sitting on the beach in front of Atlantic City's famous boardwalk. You'll note that women had to have their legs covered when in bathing gear in those days. My scalp was beginning to sprout hair again.

Below from left to right: Maxine Marx, Chico's daughter at age eight; Minnie, the consummate stage mother of the Four Marx Brothers; and yours truly at the age of five.

On the left: Here I am at the same photo session with Julius Marx, attired in his first made-to-order suit, looking more like a successful CPA than the funniest man on Broadway in 1925. At the time, he and his brothers were starring in "The Cocoanuts" at the Lyric Theatre.

Groucho, posing beside his expensive new Packard convertible in the driveway of our house, in the tony hamlet of Great Neck, Long Island. In golfing knickers, he was on his way to Lakeville Country Club, where he hoped to someday break ninety. He never did, but he did manage to break a number of golf clubs in sheer frustration.

Once, on Lakeville's water hole, he mis-hit a drive and killed one of the prized swans, which nearly got him kicked out of the club.

GROUCHO: *"I refuse to belong to any club that would have me as a member."*

The Early Hits

Groucho as Napoleon (left) as he appeared in 1923's "I'll Say She Is," outside the Walnut Street Theatre in Philadelphia. The Marx Brothers broke the box office record there and moved on to Broadway with the show in 1924. The Broadway smashes "The Cocoanuts" (1925) and "Animal Crackers," (1928) by George S. Kaufman and Morrie Ryskind, followed. The Marx Brothers' first film "The Cocoanuts" was released in 1929 by Paramount. Harpo, Chico, Zeppo and Groucho strike poses (right) between shots during 'Cocoanuts.'

ZEPPO: *"The garbageman is here."*
GROUCHO: *"Tell him we don't want any."*
— *I'll Say She Is*

Groucho relaxing between takes with my mother, Ruth, on the set of "Animal Crackers" in 1929, at the Paramount Studios lot in Astoria, Long Island, New York, where many pictures were shot in those days. Groucho wouldn't be looking so happy when the stock market crashed a few days later, wiping out his life savings of $240,000.

GROUCHO: *"I worked myself up from nothing to a state of extreme poverty."*
                                    — *The Cocoanuts*

Below, the Marx threesome mug for a publicity shot on "The Cocoanuts" set, also shot at Astoria Studios.

Rare publicity shots from the 1930 Paramount release "Animal Crackers" in which Groucho played Captain Geoffrey T. Spaulding, the African explorer. (Did someone call him 'schnorrer?' Hooray, hooray, hooray.) Featured are Louis Sorin, Groucho and Margaret Dumont - the Marxes' expert foil.

GROUCHO: *"One morning I shot an elephant in my pajamas.*
How he got in my pajamas I don't know."
— *Animal Crackers*

"He'll learn more by going to Europe than he will sitting in a school room," Groucho would tell our mother. I don't know how true that was – my grades were never that good – but I certainly saw a lot of the world. The picture on the left of Groucho, me and my mother in her first extravagant purchase, a mink coat, was taken aboard the French liner, Paris in late 1930, when the Marx Brothers were on their way to London to do their act.

On January 8, 1931, upon docking in Plymouth, England prior to their run at the Palace, the Marx Brothers, Chico, Groucho and Zeppo bid a cheerful farewell to the ship's purser. Harpo arrived by boat later.

Groucho hams it up shipboard. In 1931, we returned from Europe on the Liner Paris.

When the ship docked, all the passengers went straight through customs – including Harpo, Chico and Zeppo. But my father, my mother, Ruth, my sister Miriam and I were held up for four hours. They went through all our luggage with a fine tooth comb and made us go into separate rooms and take off all our clothes. I think it may have had something to do with the way my father filled out the customs form:

NAME: *Julius H. Marx*

ADDRESS: *21 Lincoln Road,*
Great Neck,
Long Island

HAIR: *Very little*

OCCUPATION: *Smuggler*

PURCHASES: *Wouldn't you*
like to know!

24

Groucho and Thelma Todd in 1931's "Monkey Business."
THELMA TODD: *"You're awfully shy for a lawyer."*
GROUCHO: *"You bet I'm shy. I'm a shyster lawyer."*

Uncle Harpo and I clowning around between takes on the set of "Monkey Business" in 1931. I worked as an extra on this film (I wonder how I got the job?) and earned a whopping $25 for a couple of days work in a scene that wound up on the cutting room floor. At the time, a friend and I used to roller-skate past street lights in Hollywoodland, where we lived, and tried to see how many we could break by throwing rocks at them. I broke the most street lights, and was pretty proud of this accomplishment until a gendarme showed up at our front door one day and arrested me for destroying city property. I wasn't put in reform school, but I was fined $25. There went the pay for my day's work in "Monkey Business."

Groucho, the movie star, on the Paramount lot in 1931 during the filming of "Monkey Business." Here he is flanked by my four year-old sister Miriam, our mother Ruth, and "Monkey Business" screenwriter Arthur Sheekman — one of my father's life-long friends — taking a stroll after a bad lunch in the Paramount commissary in Hollywood.

Zeppo, actress Ruth Hall, Harpo, Chico and Groucho on the set of "Monkey Business."

Pictured on the left are Groucho and my mother with comedian Charlie Butterworth and his lovely wife Ethel at a 1933 costume party. Groucho took pride in going as the rear-end of Rex the Wonder Horse.

On the right is a rare photo of my aunt Marion (Zeppo's wife) and my father at a Gay Nineties Party hosted by fellow Paramount player Frederic March in 1932.

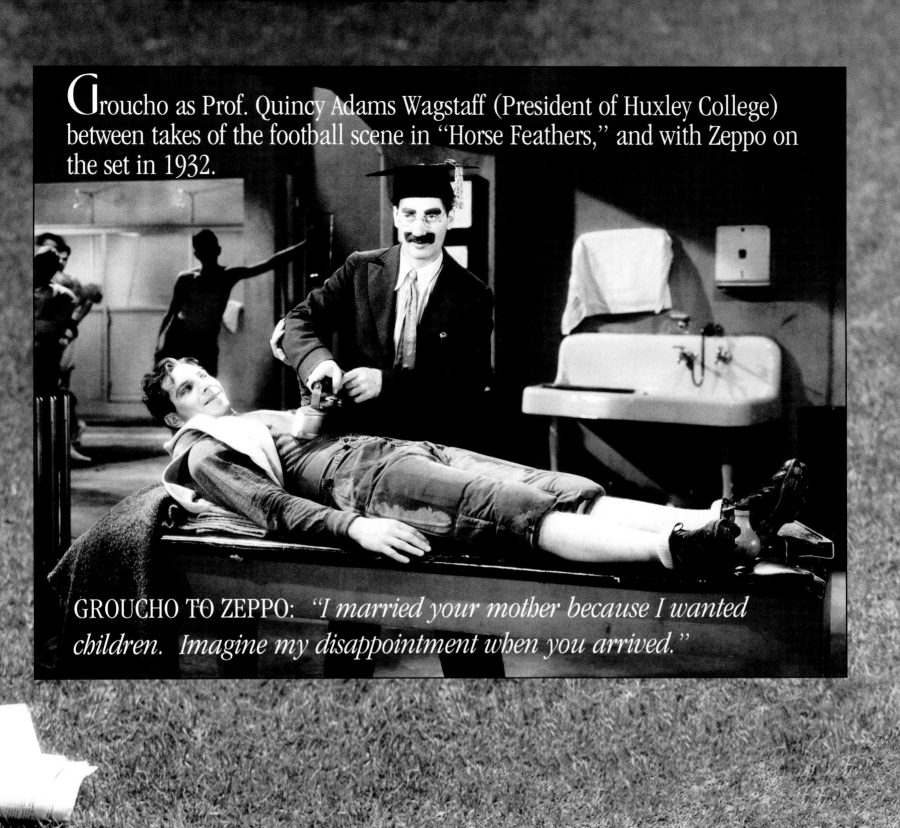

Groucho as Prof. Quincy Adams Wagstaff (President of Huxley College) between takes of the football scene in "Horse Feathers," and with Zeppo on the set in 1932.

GROUCHO TO ZEPPO: *"I married your mother because I wanted children. Imagine my disappointment when you arrived."*

This photo titled "Our Meschpoche" captures the Marx and Schoenberg family reunion on January 8, 1932 at the Croydon Hotel in New York. Seated around the table from left to right are Johanna Shean (Al's wife); their son Larry; the Marxes' father Sam Marx; Tante Sarah; Chico; Tante Hannah Schickler; Uncle Al Shean; Harpo; another Tante Sarah; Chico's daughter Maxine; Heine Schoenberg; his son; Chico's mother-in-law (Mrs. Sarah Karp); Cousin Polly Muller; her husband Sam; the hotel waiter (standing); five unidentified relatives; Zeppo; another unidentified relative; Beattie Muller (Polly's daughter); Groucho; mother Ruth; Zeppo's wife Marion; Chico's wife Betty; Gummo's wife Helen; Gummo; and four unidentified relatives.

OUR MESCHPOCHE

After immortalizing their footprints in cement outside Grauman's Chinese Theatre in 1933, Groucho, Harpo, Chico, Sid Grauman and Zeppo parade in kilts amongst their fans along Hollywood Boulevard.

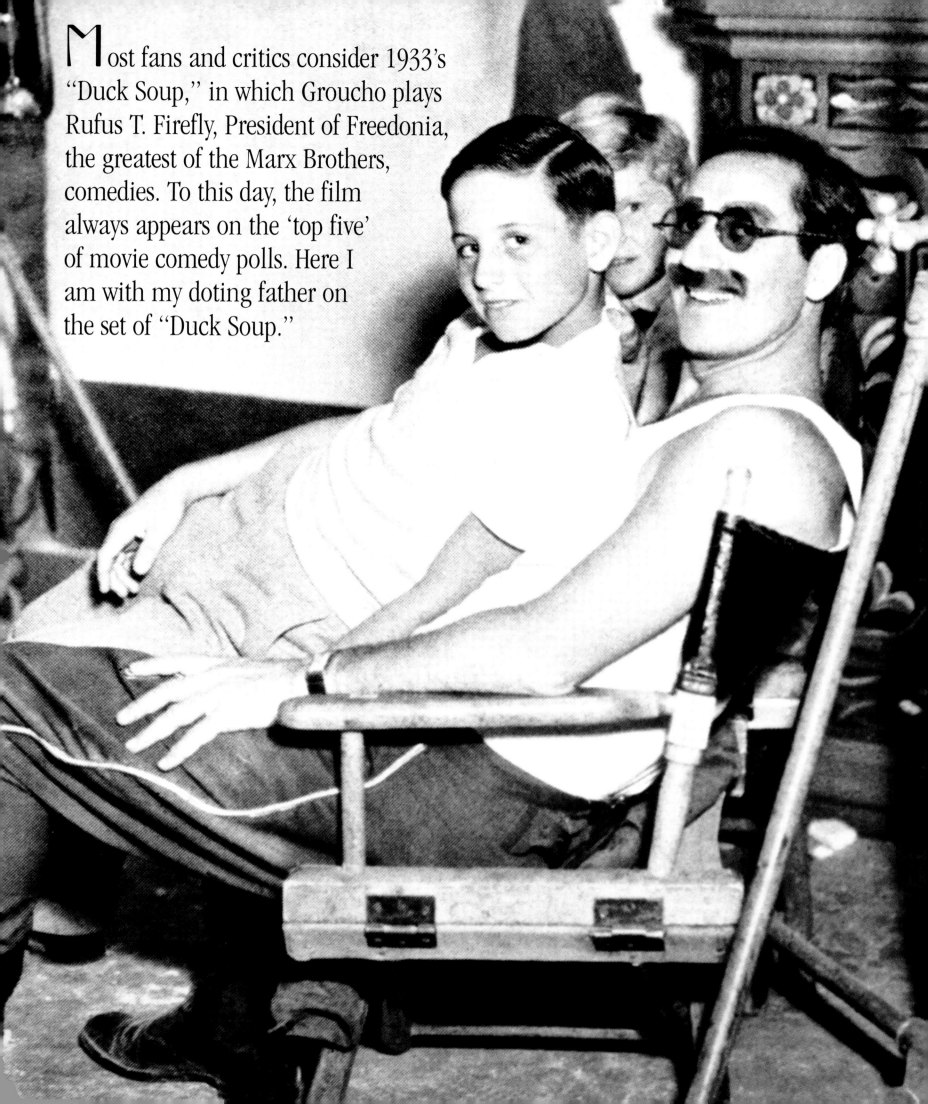

Most fans and critics consider 1933's "Duck Soup," in which Groucho plays Rufus T. Firefly, President of Freedonia, the greatest of the Marx Brothers, comedies. To this day, the film always appears on the 'top five' of movie comedy polls. Here I am with my doting father on the set of "Duck Soup."

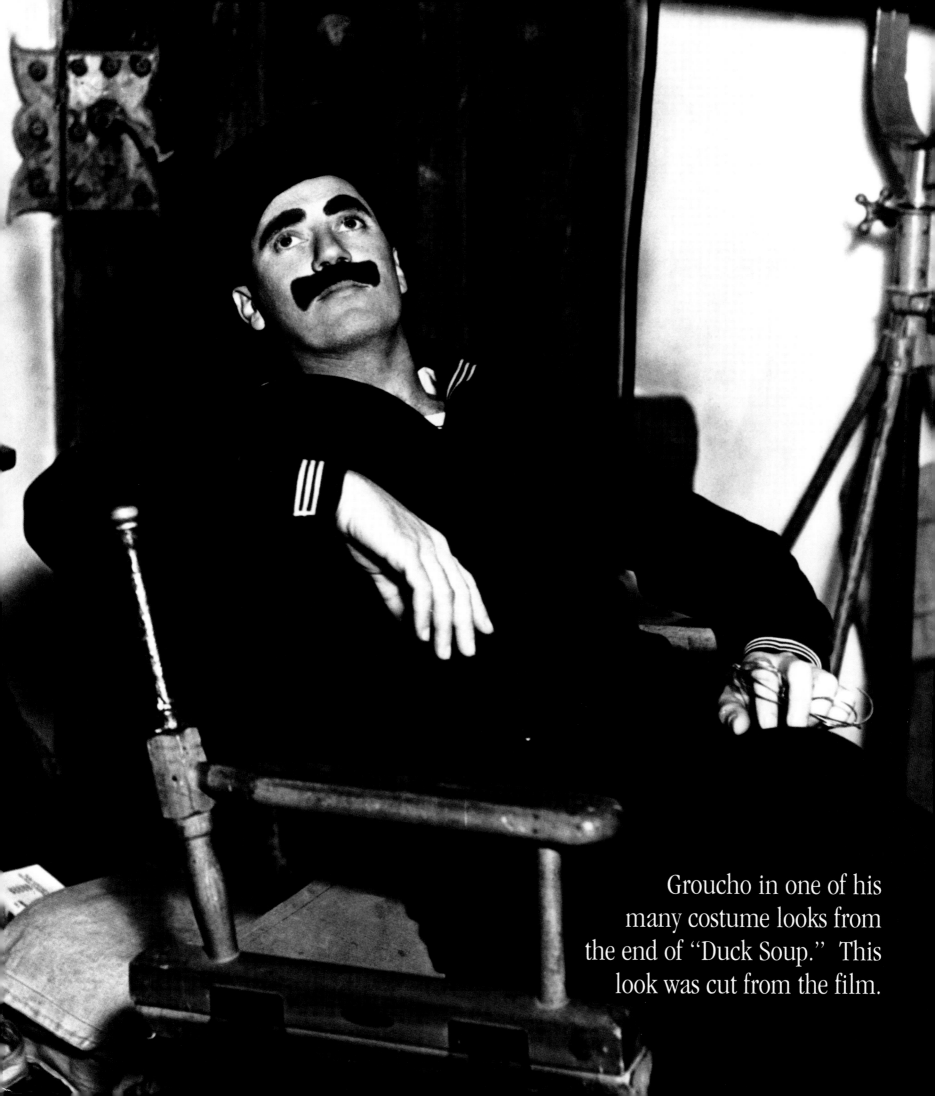

Groucho in one of his many costume looks from the end of "Duck Soup." This look was cut from the film.

On the Paramount lot in 1933 are Groucho, Jackie Cooper, Carole Lombard and Harpo (left).

On the set of "Duck Soup" with my mother Ruth, sister Miriam, Dad, Uncle Harpo and an unidentified chimp (above).

GROUCHO (TO MARGARET DUMONT): *"I can see you in the kitchen right now bending over a hot stove. But I can't see the stove."*

— *Duck Soup*

Chico and Groucho play lawyers in the 1934 CBS radio show "Flywheel, Shyster and Flywheel" penned by Marx writers Nat Perrin and Arthur Sheekman.

GROUCHO TO CHICO: *"You know I could rent you out as a decoy for duck hunters."*

And, as they appeared outside court three years later defending themselves against copyright infringement charges for said show. The case was settled out of court.

Between takes of "A Night at the Opera" with composer Gus Kahn, Groucho, Harpo blowing smoke bubbles, comedian Ted Healy (the Three Stooges' original straight man), Chico and Ben Bernie, the famous orchestra leader.

MARGARET DUMONT: *"Are you sure you have everything, Otis."*

GROUCHO: *I haven't had any complaints yet."*

Chico, Groucho and Harpo strangle director Sam Wood. And, according to my father for good reason. Groucho despised Sam Wood and his insistence on shooting scenes forty times each. After Groucho muffed a line during a take, Wood exclaimed, "Well, you can't make an actor out of clay." To which Groucho shot back, "Nor a director out of Wood."

Director Sam Wood behind the camera shooting another take of a complicated farcical scene from "A Night at the Opera."

When I was growing up, I was always asked, "Is your father as funny at home as he is in the movies?" I believe this picture (circa 1934) answers that. However, when he wasn't clowning, he was an excellent pool player, as were Chico, Harpo and Zeppo.

The Marx Family at Home

This is the house where I grew up after we moved to Beverly Hills from the East. It's still there, in the seven hundred block of Hillcrest Road. When my father bought it in 1933, there were five empty lots from our house to Sunset Boulevard. At the time, it was rumored that those lots would never be sold, because their owner was asking $7,500 apiece for them. Those rumors turned out to be incorrect.

In my mother's sewing room was a walk-in safe in which my father kept the .32 caliber revolver he owned. Since he never knew the combination to the safe, no one, including burglars, had to worry about being shot.

51

This year I discovered, along with my existing negatives, ten three-minute 16mm home movie reels dating back to 1935. Here Groucho is captured at home in a T-shirt, smoking a pipe. According to Smithsonian sources, the films are beyond restoration, but can be re-animated through computer technology. Some images that can be seen by the naked eye include Groucho playing guitar, Miriam at the piano and me playing tennis. Who knows what Marxian antics remain to be viewed.

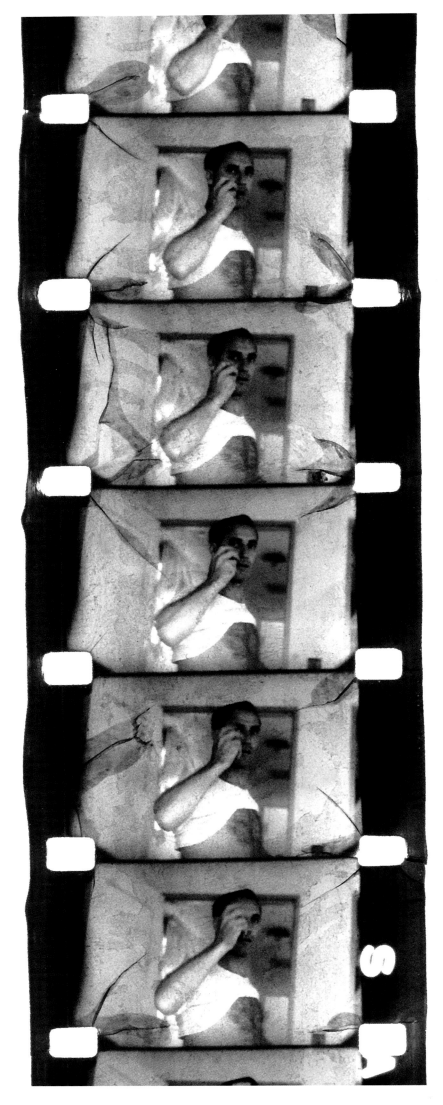

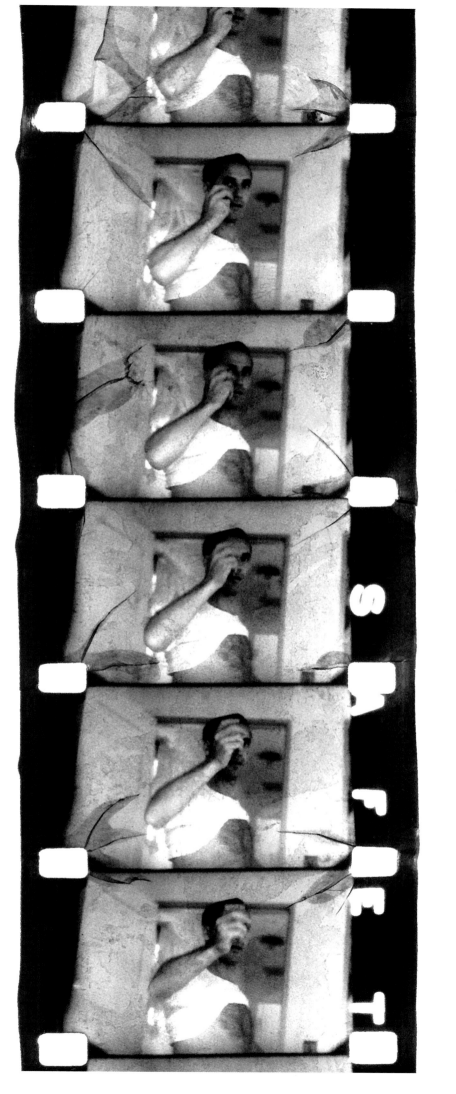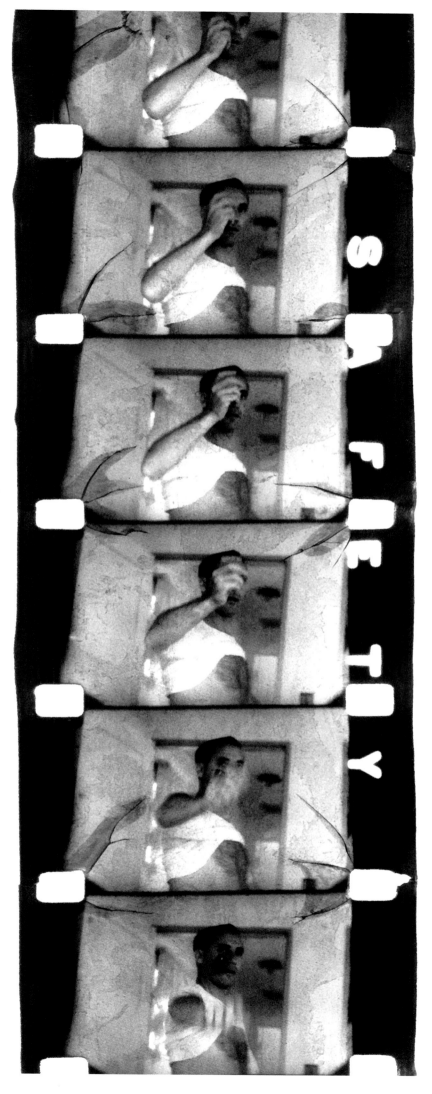

Groucho was a homebody. Twenty-five years of touring every crummy town in the nation will do that to you. My mother loved to go out dancing, but Dad preferred to stay home and listen to records on his beloved Capehart, smoke his pipe and read a good book.

These are pictures I took in the living room of our Beverly Hills house in 1935. The bottom photo shows one of the rare times I was able to capture him on film smoking a pipe.

Groucho was an avid reader and never without a book in his hand. He even ke[pt] books in his car, along with a Webster's Dictionary, which he referred to if he chance[d] to run across a word he didn't know the meaning of. Above (right) is a candid shot [I] took of my father reading a newspaper when he was in Skowhegan, Maine in 193[4] where he was playing the lead on stage in "On the Twentieth Century." He even rea[d] while shaving with his electric razor. But it wasn't until I took the shot on the rig[ht] that I first knew he could read a newspaper in his sleep.

GROUCHO: "Outside of a dog, a man's best friend is a book; inside of a dog,

Every evening before dinner, our entire family gathered around the piano and had a spirited musicale, the well-known theory being that a family that plays together stays together. On the left and below are photos of Father practicing guitar.

59

My father and his guitar teacher, Bill Mathes, are seen below in a picture taken in the den off Groucho's bedroom. Although Father taught himself to play the guitar by ear when he was in vaudeville, he felt he'd be a better musician if he could read music. So, he started taking lessons and practiced diligently for a couple of hours everyday. Besides learning how to read popular sheet music, he delved into the classics and eventually could play Rachmaninoff's Prelude in C Sharp Minor, which had originally been written for the piano. I'm no music critic, but I can tell you it sounded better when Rachmaninoff played it on the piano.

Groucho took his guitar playing so seriously that he cultivated a friendship with Andre Segovia, the late, great classical guitarist. Groucho had him to dinner at our house one night with Max Gordon, the Broadway producer responsible for "Born Yesterday," among a great many other Broadway shows. Segovia was middle-aged, very dignified and not too conversant with the English language. Gordon on the other hand was boisterous and crude, a fellow who always got right to the point. During dinner, Gordon asked Segovia what he did for a living. Segovia told him that he went around the world giving guitar concerts in places like Carnegie Hall, Albert Hall in London, etc. Fascinated, Gordon, who'd started out as a vaudeville booking agent, listened attentively until Segovia finished his speech. At this point he turned to Segovia and said, without meaning to be funny, "Sounds like one night stands with a banjo."

Miriam and Groucho having lunch on our screened-in porch. From the expression on Miriam's face, he obviously is telling her to eat her spinach or she wouldn't get any dessert. Note Groucho's suspenders. He was way ahead of Larry King in that regard. On the right, Miriam is shown choosing what she wants for Christmas, and dressed as Annie Oakley with our dog, Shep – an Australian sheep dog that was given to my father and me at a cattle ranch in Northern California when he was four weeks old.

Groucho in bathrobe and pajamas in our breakfast room, enjoying the same breakfast that he'd been eating for the past twenty years — half a grapefruit, two pieces of toast and coffee.

Miriam photographing Groucho while I photographed the two of them. After he saw this picture, he went on a diet, weighed himself daily and kept track of his weight on a chart. If he gained a pound, he would only have one slice of pumpernickel for lunch. If he lost a pound or two, he'd treat himself to a chocolate soda at Martha Smith's, a popular ice cream and soda joint on Beverly Drive.

One of the great things about having Groucho for a father was that he never wanted to take a trip unless he could bring his kids along. Here are Groucho and Miriam in the patio of the Hotel Agua Caliente in Baja California. He enjoyed visiting Mexico, because he liked getting heartburn while eating chile con carne. He said the heartburn

made him feel young again, because it reminded him of when he was a boy, playing small time vaudeville along the border towns in Texas. There he was forced to partake of his meals in greasy spoon joints, where "The safest things to order," he said, "were a coconut, a hard-boiled egg and a banana."

Mother and Father enjoying a lively game of ping-pong on our screened porch. There was always a great rivalry between them when it came to racquet sports. She was the better of the two at ping-pong and tennis, but he usually wound up defeating her because he'd make her laugh and she'd lose her concentration. On the left, Miriam and I wield our paddles in self-defense.

Groucho at Santa Anita Race Track in the mid-Thirties (on the left). He didn't like horse racing or any kind of gambling, so I must have taken this of him at the race track while he was filming "A Day at the Races."

The famous Chico smile (above), which no woman could resist. His wife Betty stayed married to him for thirty years, in spite of the fact that he was an incorrigible gambler and womanizer. When Betty walked in on Chico with another woman, he had a perfect explanation, "I was just whispering in her mouth."

On the Set
Maureen O'Sullivan, Margaret Dumont, Groucho and Chico (far right) in gondola sequence from "A Day at the Races."

Groucho had a crush on O'Sullivan, who played the love interest in the picture opposite Allan Jones. Maureen was married at the time. If my father had been anything like his brother Chico, he wouldn't have let that stop him from pursuing her seriously. But since he was Groucho, he just yearned for her quietly.

Here I caught Groucho sitting in director Sam Wood's chair. He's smiling, so he must not have had an argument with the director that day, or had to bawl out his brother Chico for not bothering to learn his lines before coming to the studio. Note Groucho's self-annotated script.

Chico and Harpo wait for the
Venetian Waters scene to be shot.

ESTHER MUIR: *"I've never been so insulted in my life."*
GROUCHO: *"We'll, it's early yet."*
—*A Day at the Races*

Groucho and Chico between takes on the set of 'Races,' which was filmed in 1937.

Between scenes playing
Dr. Hugo Z. Hackenbush,
Groucho enjoys an
ice cream break.

Here I captured the film's big dance number, with all the stable hands and their children singing and dancing to "All God's Children Got Rhythm."

Chico on High Hat (left), the race horse that everyone hoped would win, and did, in order to save Margaret Dumont's sanitarium from being taken over by the villains. According to my father, "Even though Chico had read the script and knew how the race was going to turn out, he still bet on the wrong horse."

These photos were taken by me just prior to the big race in "A Day at the Races." Chico's riding outfit was a look that was later cut from the film.

The unflappable Margaret Dumont on the set of "A Day at the Races" (below), and in a scene (right) from "Animal Crackers." Many referred to her as the fifth Marx Brother. In seven Marx films she played the society dowager put upon by Groucho.

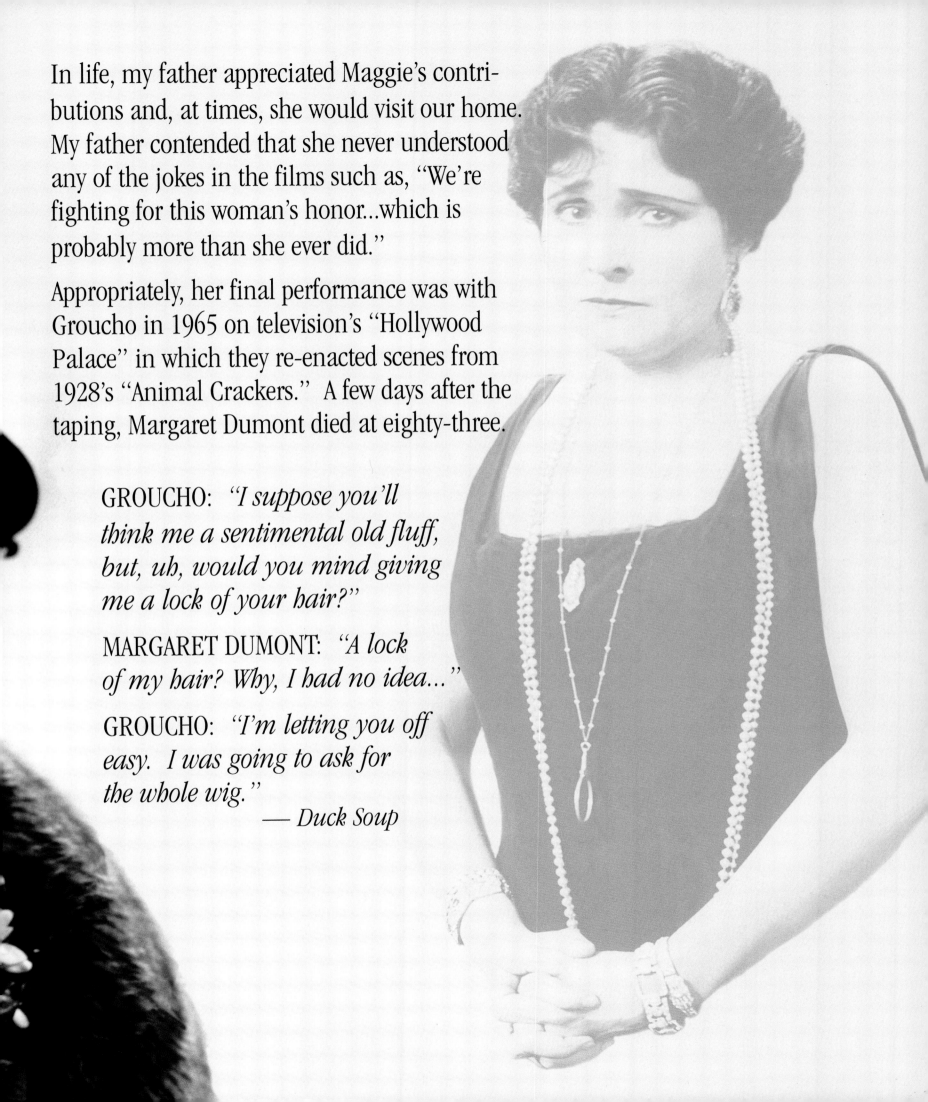

In life, my father appreciated Maggie's contributions and, at times, she would visit our home. My father contended that she never understood any of the jokes in the films such as, "We're fighting for this woman's honor...which is probably more than she ever did."

Appropriately, her final performance was with Groucho in 1965 on television's "Hollywood Palace" in which they re-enacted scenes from 1928's "Animal Crackers." A few days after the taping, Margaret Dumont died at eighty-three.

GROUCHO: *"I suppose you'll think me a sentimental old fluff, but, uh, would you mind giving me a lock of your hair?"*

MARGARET DUMONT: *"A lock of my hair? Why, I had no idea..."*

GROUCHO: *"I'm letting you off easy. I was going to ask for the whole wig."*
— *Duck Soup*

Father strums the guitar next to 'Races' composer Gus Kahn.

Kahn wrote such standards as "Makin' Whoopee" and "It Had To Be You."

Note Harpo's stand-in smoking a pipe in the background.

Mother outside our home opening the door of our new La Salle. We once received a car from the Dodge Brothers as the result of a punch-line delivered by Groucho in "A Day at the Races."

1st DOCTOR: *(introducing himself)*: *"Johnson, Bellevue, 1918."*
2nd DOCTOR: *"Franco, John Hopkins, '22"*
3rd DOCTOR: *"Wilmerding, Mayo Brothers, '24."*
GROUCHO: *"Dodge Brothers, late '29."*

Zeppo quit being a Marx Brother in 1935 and became a powerful Hollywood agent whose clients were among the biggest stars in Hollywood – Clark Gable, Carole Lombard, Robert Taylor, Barbara Stanwyck and the Marx Brothers, just to mention a few. After his agency became extremely successful, he took in his brother Gummo as a partner. The two of them developed the Marx agency into one of the most influential in Hollywood, with a fancy suite of offices on the Sunset Strip. With Gummo taking some of the burden of running the agency off Zeppo's shoulders, he branched out into other ventures – a factory that manufactured airplane parts for the war effort during World War II and a race horse breeding ranch in the San Fernando Valley. Zeppo's partner in both these profitable enterprises was screen star Robert Taylor (husband of Barbara Stanwyck). The name of the ranch was Marwyck.

Below: Zeppo, the horseman, aboard one of his favorite mounts. On the right: My father and mother being shown around the ranch by Zeppo. In the bottom right photo (left to right) are my mother, Zeppo, Groucho and Mrs. Bimberg, (Marion's mother) sitting in front of one of the barns.

GROUCHO: *"I'd horsewhip you if I had a horse."*   — *Horse Feathers*

Rare shots of all five Marx Brothers together, taken in Groucho's Beverly Hills home circa 1938. At this time, Zeppo was representing the Marx Brothers for their next film, "Room Service." Standing from left to right: Zeppo, Groucho, Chico, Gummo and Harpo.

GROUCHO (referring to Harpo): "This is Mr. Englund, the brains of the organization. That'll give you an idea of the organization."

Harpo, Chico and Groucho pose for a publicity shot as bellboys for 1938's "Room Service." Lucille Ball and Ann Miller co-starred. A publicity pose with a Marx foil (top left), and with director William Seiter and Pandro Berman who produced many of Astaire and Rogers' classic musical films (bottom).

Daughter Miriam with her father on a location set of 1939's "At the Circus," in which he sang "Lydia, the Tattooed Lady."

GROUCHO: *"Ah, Lydia. I met her in 1900, marked down from 1940."*

FP5

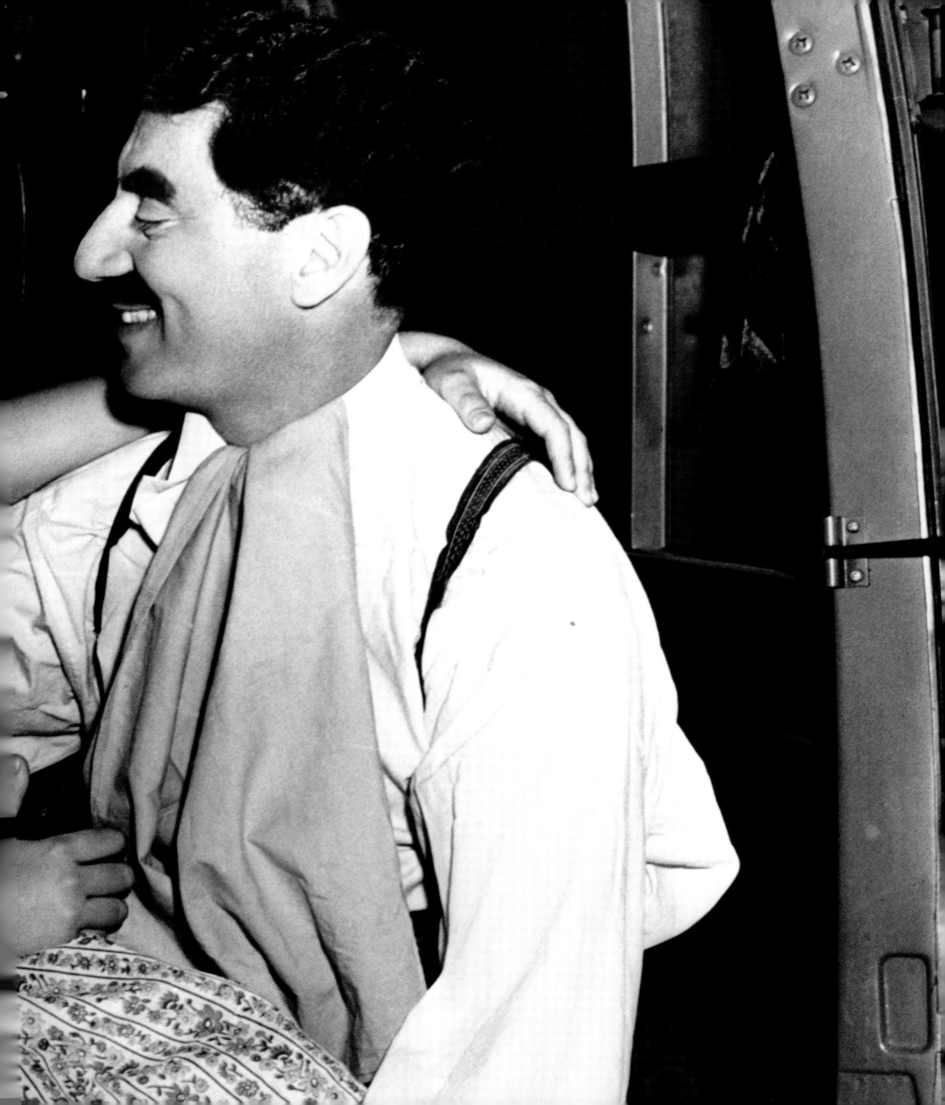

S. Quentin Quale as portrayed by Groucho in 1940's "Go West" (right).

Ingenue Diana Lewis, Groucho, Chico and Harpo pose for an MGM publicity shot.

Tennis, Anyone?

From the time I was ten years old until I left home to go into the service during World War II, my life and the rest of my family's, revolved around tennis. My mother and father had been tennis hackers in the East. They weren't very good, but they took me in hand to teach me the rudiments. By the time I was 13, I could beat every grown-up who frequented Harpo's court down the street from our house in Beverly Hills.

In this photo taken on June 16, 1935, Dad shows off his form at the Beverly Hills Tennis Club, which he joined to further my tennis career.

At the Beverly Hills Tennis Club, Groucho demonstrates his unique overhead smash.

And demonstrates how to prevent catching a cold after a brisk workout.

A topless, hairy-chested Groucho getting ready to master the courts at the Beverly Hills Tennis Club. Groucho was a typical duffer. He had a weak serve, not much of a backhand or net game, but he had a fairly strong forehand which he kiddingly referred to as Iron Mike. Whenever he played singles with my mother, who was actually a better player than he was, he'd always say something during the match when he was losing that would upset her. Like, "Watch out, Ruth. I'm going to give you Iron Mike." She scoffed at this threat, but then managed to net the next shot, and eventually he'd walk off the court the winner.

On the left, my mother and father rest on their racquets between points on the tennis court at the North Shore Tavern at Lake Arrowhead, California.

Marx of U. S. C. Halts McGehee in 4 Sets

By LOUIS EFFRAT
Special to THE NEW YORK TIMES.

By 1939, I was ranked fifth in the National 18-and-under. In 1940, I won the Eastern Junior College and Freshman Tournament at Montclair, New Jersey and was runner-up to Bobby Riggs (the reigning Wimbledon champ) in the finals of the Tri-State in Cincinnati. And, I also did the unthinkable…I defeated the great Jack Kramer. ("It was the low point of my tennis career," remembers Kramer with a grimace.) In 1941, I retired from tennis to take a job in radio, writing jokes for Milton Berle. My father made me quit tennis because, he told me, "There's no money in it." That's known as being born fifty years too soon. But I don't regret it. I'd never have known my father if I hadn't been born when I was.

And Takes Eastern Freshman Tennis Title

My mother coping with the boredom of being a tennis parent, in our hotel room at the Hotel Valencia in La Jolla, California, where I was competing in one of my first junior tennis tournaments. Before I had a driver's license and a car, Mother schlepped me to all the tennis tournaments around Southern California.

Pictured left to right are Miriam Schary, Dore's wife; Dore Schary, who replaced Louis B. Mayer as head of production at MGM Studios; and Groucho and my mother at the Beverly Hills Tennis Club's barn dance. Groucho hated parties and only went because my mother made him. The following is an excerpt from a letter he wrote me when I was away in the East playing the tennis circuit.

"*Last night the club threw its barn dance, and surprisingly enough it was a big success. They had ninety people, a good band, and open air dancing around the pool. The catering was delegated to Levitoff the pastrami prince, and the crowd ate like wolves and drank like stevedores. If it weren't for the police, the party would still be going, but at the fatal hour of two the cops arrived, brandishing their clubs and announced that the band would have to cease firing or continue playing at the local jail. This sent most of the members to the bar, but the departure of the musicians dampened the ardor of the survivors and shortly after that they began wending their way homeward. That was quite a blow to many of them as home is something they don't like to contemplate.*

The disturbing phase of the party is the fact that because of its success the girls are already beginning to discuss the next one, whether to have white tie and tails or have everybody come as coal miners. At any rate, the club cleared a nice profit at the bar. Many of the members, including your mother, decided to try to drink the club out of its deficit, and with the help of a few guests, who also gave up their kidneys for the good of the club, a healthy profit was cleared."

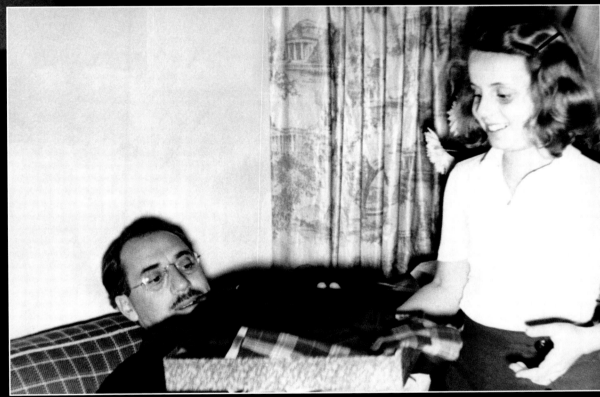

Christmas at the Marxes
Groucho hosts a 1941 Christmas party in our den. In the lower right are Janet Oswald, Miriam's best friend who lived next door and Miriam's forehead. Directly above, Groucho receives a lap full of presents that he would be returning as soon as the stores opened the next day. This would be one of the last holidays my mother and father would spend together.

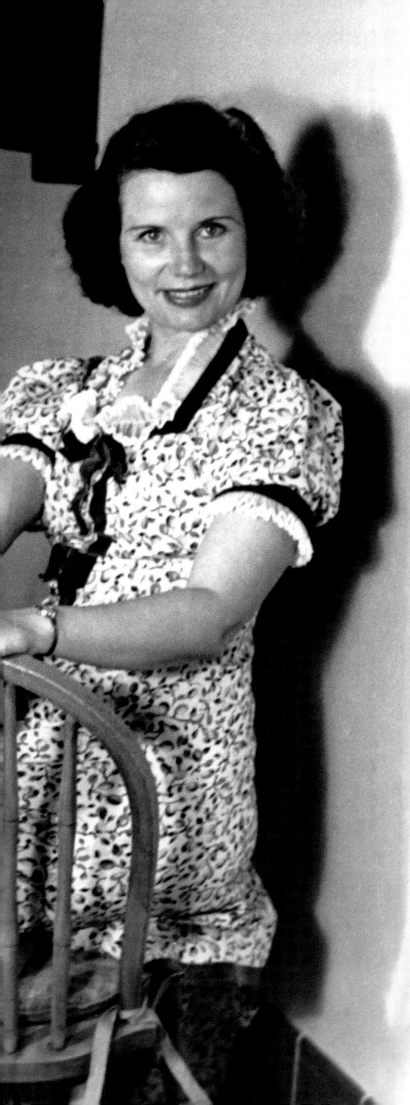

My mother was a true beauty. She met my father in 1918 when they were playing at the Palace Theatre in "Home Again." She was a dancer in the act and performed an adagio with my Uncle Zeppo. It was one of the major disappointments of her life that my father made her quit show business when they were still in vaudeville. At the age of thirty-seven (on the right), she looked better than most of today's glamour girls.

After twenty-two years of marriage, my parents went their separate ways. They were never well-suited for each other. As the years passed, their differences became even more evident. Father's impatience and caustic remarks heightened as my mother's drinking progressed. In 1942, my father described to me the final awkward moment with my mother. It was one of those half serious, half comic moments. As he walked her to her car he put out his hand and said, "Ruth, it was nice knowing you, and if you're ever in the neighborhood again, drop in." It was ironic. In the last moment of their relationship, he finally got a laugh from his wife.

Groucho as attorney Wolf J. Flywheel in 1941's "The Big Store." The Marx Brothers announced their retirement from the screen after this film.

GROUCHO: *"Martha, dear, there are many bonds that will hold us together through eternity."*

MARGARET DUMONT: *"Really, Wolf, what are they?"*

GROUCHO: *"Your government bonds, your savings bonds, your Liberty Bonds..."*

Groucho, smoking his after-lunch Dunhill cigar (on the left) circa 1941. Contrary to popular legend, he only smoked two cigars a day – one after lunch and the other after dinner. In between cigars he smoked a pipe, but never touched a cigarette unless he was desperate for a smoke and didn't have a cigar or pipe on him. Without cigar or mustache, he seldom was taken for the great comedian known to the public. "I just look like a middle-aged Jew," he told me when I showed him the snapshot.

Another portrait (above) of Groucho at home, by yours truly. Note the real mustache beneath the greasepaint. He was experimenting with a real one because he hated the greasepaint he wore on the stage and in the movies, and wanted to see if audiences would accept him without the phony one. At the time, he was considering dissolving the Marx act and launching a radio career, which he thought was a lot easier way of making a living, because in radio he didn't have to wear a costume or memorize any lines. He got his wish years later when "You Bet Your Life" became a hit.

The King of Comedy with the Queen of Comedy, Lucille Ball, in the early 1940's.

GROUCHO AT WAR

Although my father never ventured overseas to do any troop entertaining during World War II, he did his bit for his country by playing all the Army and Navy and Air Force camps in this country. He also did a lot of broadcasting for Armed Forces Radio and made appearances at the local USO's around Southern California. Once he was doing a show from Camp Pendleton, the Marine Base down near San Diego, and found himself sitting in the Commanding General's office, waiting to go on. When the phone rang on the General's desk, Groucho picked up the receiver, and said, "World War II speaking."

Pictured here are Groucho, guest star Ginger Rogers and her husband Capt. Jack Briggs at Camp Pendleton where Groucho performed.

GROUCHO: *"Military intelligence is a contradiction in terms."*

The Hollywood Victory Caravan crossed the country by train in 1942. By the time the bandwagon of performing stars reached Minneapolis, forty million dollars had been raised for the war effort. In this photograph are Groucho, Desi Arnaz, Pat O'Brien, Bert Lahr,

Oliver Hardy, Jerry Colonna, Cary Grant, Joan Blondell, Frank McHugh, Risé Stevens, Claudette Colbert, Fay McKenzie, Charlotte Greenwood, Frances Langford, Edward Arnold, Charles Boyer, Eleanor Powell, Joan Bennett and Olivia de Havilland.

Musical shenanigans on the Victory Caravan. Photo includes Cary Grant on drums, Joan Blondell on trumpet, Groucho on sax and Bert Lahr on bass

Another Caravan shot featuring James Cagney, Stan Laurel, Frances Langford, Pat O'Brien, Frank McHugh, Charlotte Greenwood, Risé Stevens and Groucho at piano.

The Caravan stopped in Washington, D.C. to meet up with First Lady Eleanor Roosevelt. Additional members pictured include Merle Oberon and Bob Hope.

ELEANOR ROOSEVELT: *"I'm very happy to meet you, Mr. Marx."*
GROUCHO: *"Are we late for dinner?"*

Once asked by *Parade Magazine* who the funniest man in the world is, Bob Hope responded, "Fellow comedians – myself included – are all openly and vociferously envious of Groucho Marx. I'll take Groucho because of his unfailing wit..."

Groucho: "Bob has the best delivery. He's the All-American boy."

RADIO Groucho finally had brief success on CBS radio as star of "Pabst Blue Ribbon Town." Here's Father high-kicking with show regular Fay McKenzie and Carole Landis during a rehearsal for the Pabst program broadcast.

Dorothy Lamour (left) woos Groucho on the Pabst show. Chico and Father court Carole Lombard (right) after her guest appearance on The Kellogg Hour radio program in 1939.

During the war, my ship was stationed on the Island of Leyte, a rather remote section of the Philippines where none of the big entertainers ventured. For that reason an entertainment unit was assembled, and I was chosen to put a show together because the Commander had noticed in my service record that I had once written comedy scripts for Milton Berle. Although I never imitated Groucho in our show, in a moment of extreme weakness I allowed a Coast Guard PR photographer to talk me into having my picture taken wearing a black greasepaint mustache, steel-rimmed spectacles and a pith helmet – a lá Captain Spaulding in "Animal Crackers."

And, of course, the likeness wouldn't have been complete without the long cigar in my mouth. The picture made all the newspaper wire services back in the States on July 13, 1945, and under it was the following caption: "Coast Guardsman Arthur J. Marx, son of the celebrated comedian, Groucho Marx, not only resembles his father in appearance but also authors an entertaining radio program at a Coast Guard base in the Philippines which is heard in most parts of the Southwest Pacific over an Armed Forces Radio Station. The former college racquet star wears the Philippine Liberation Ribbon, and calls Beverly Hills, California home." In the next mail that came from Stateside was a letter from my father, which read:

"Dear Big Feet, I see by the newspaper that you are stealing my act.
If you don't cut it out I will be forced to sue you. Love, Doctor Hackenbush"

During this period, my father had to be in New York on business. One day while strolling through Times Square, he bumped into Max Gordon, the legendary Broadway producer who was a close friend of his. Without fail, Gordon, as usual, launched into a speech about how the legitimate theater was being ruined by the critics. Groucho listened to his tirade for about ten minutes, then said very angrily, "Listen, Max, I don't give a damn about what's wrong with the legitimate theater while this war is going on. Do you realize I have a son who is in the South Pacific, and that he might be killed any moment, and you haven't even had the decency to ask me, 'How's Arthur?' If you were any kind of a man, you'd be interested in how he's getting along, and maybe even send him a box of cigars." Gordon let him finish, then launched right back into what was wrong with the legitimate theater. Finally, Groucho cut him off mid-sentence and said, "Well, I have to get going, Max. I've had enough of your problems. See ya." They shook hands, and as Gordon started to walk away, he wheeled around and asked, "By the way, Groucho, how's Arthur?" A few weeks later, while I was still stationed in the Philippines, I opened a package that had arrived for me in the mail, and discovered it to be a box of expensive Dunhill cigars, with a note that simply said:

"Love, Max."

I'm still puzzled.

The photo on the left was taken on the set of "A Night in Casablanca" the day I arrived in Los Angeles after my sixteen-month sojourn in the South Pacific. Coast Guardsman Bob Howard, on the right, was the comic from my show.

Pictured below are Miriam, me in my Yeoman 3rd Class uniform, and my father having a songfest on one of my liberties before I was shipped to Alameda Naval Air Station — and then overseas aboard a U.S. Army Repair Ship.

In 1943, Groucho met singer / dancer Catherine Mavis Gorcey, a.k.a. Kay. In 1945, they married. My father was 55, Kay was 24. They divorced a few years later. Kay had formerly been married to Leo Gorcey of the Dead End Kids. Melinda was born to Kay and Groucho in 1946.

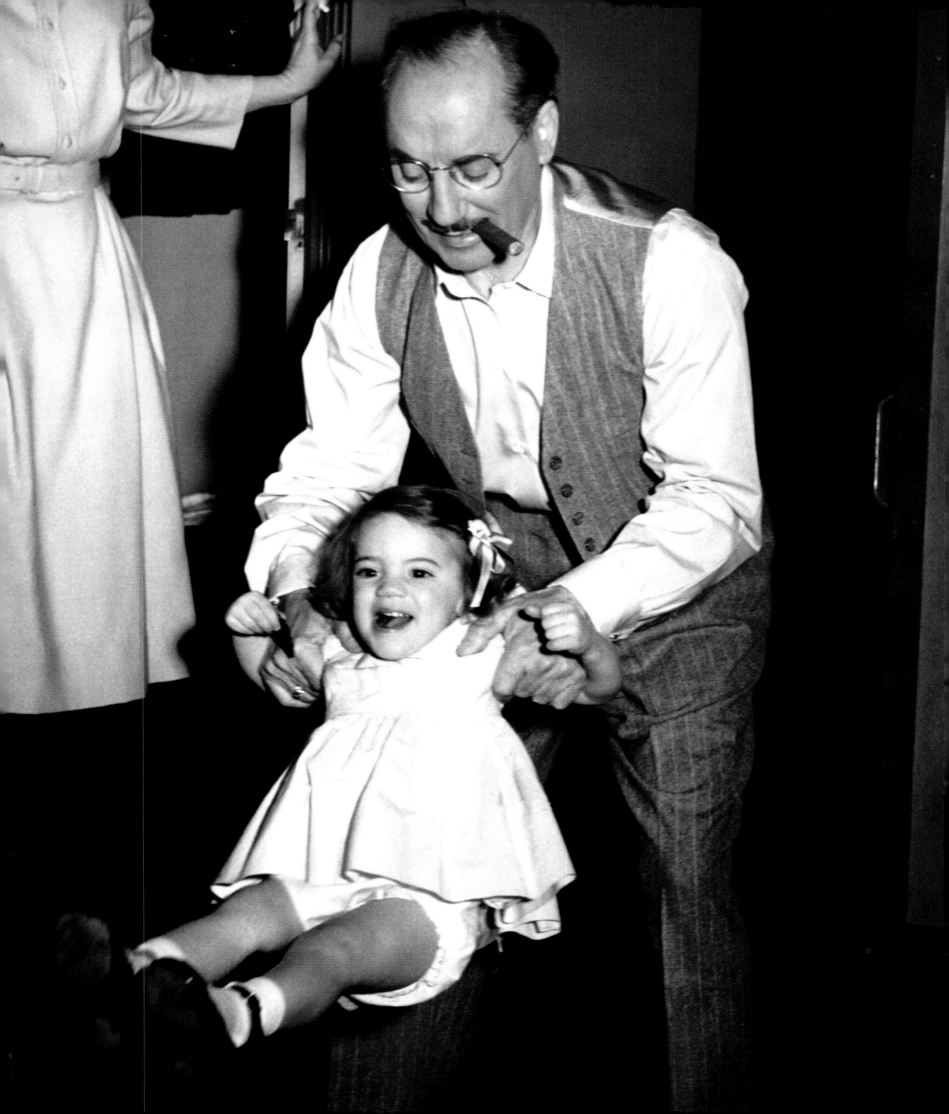

In 1946, the Marx Brothers reunited for "A Night in Casablanca" to help pay off Chico's gambling debts. Directed by Archie Mayo, the film's cast included Lisette Verea and Sigfried Rumann, with Groucho in the role of Ronald Kornblow.

BEATRICE: *"I'm Beatrice Reiner. I stop at the hotel."*

GROUCHO: *"I'm Ronald Kornblow. I stop at nothing."*

In 1947, Groucho starred in his first film effort, "Copacabana," without his brothers. Carmen Miranda co-starred, and Kay played a small part in the film (right).

GROUCHO: *"I played second banana to the fruit on Carmen Miranda's head."*

ABC's ANSWER TO INCOME TAXES...

"GIVE-AWAY" GROUCHO MARX

I AIN'T GONNA TELL YA THE SECRET WORD... I CAN'T PRONOUNCE IT!

HIS PROGRAM FEATURES A "SECRET WORD" THAT PAYS OFF BIG DOUGH

BACH—

HE NEVER DID CATCH THOSE BLONDS IN THE MOVIES...

AND HE DOESN'T ON HIS AIR-SHOW EITHER!!!

HE FIRST SLAPPED ON HIS FAMOUS GREASE-PAINT MUSTACHE IN 1927 WHEN HE DIDN'T HAVE TIME TO PUT ON HIS REGULAR FALSE ONE

After years struggling as a solo act, Groucho finally hit pay dirt with his successful radio and television comedy/quiz show "You Bet Your Life." It debuted on ABC radio in 1947, moved to CBS, and then landed a ten-year run on NBC television beginning in 1950. Always in the top ten, "You Bet Your Life" introduced the country to the 'secret word,' a falling duck and announcer/sidekick George Fenneman (pictured above).

GROUCHO (To a tree surgeon): "Have you ever fallen out of a patient."

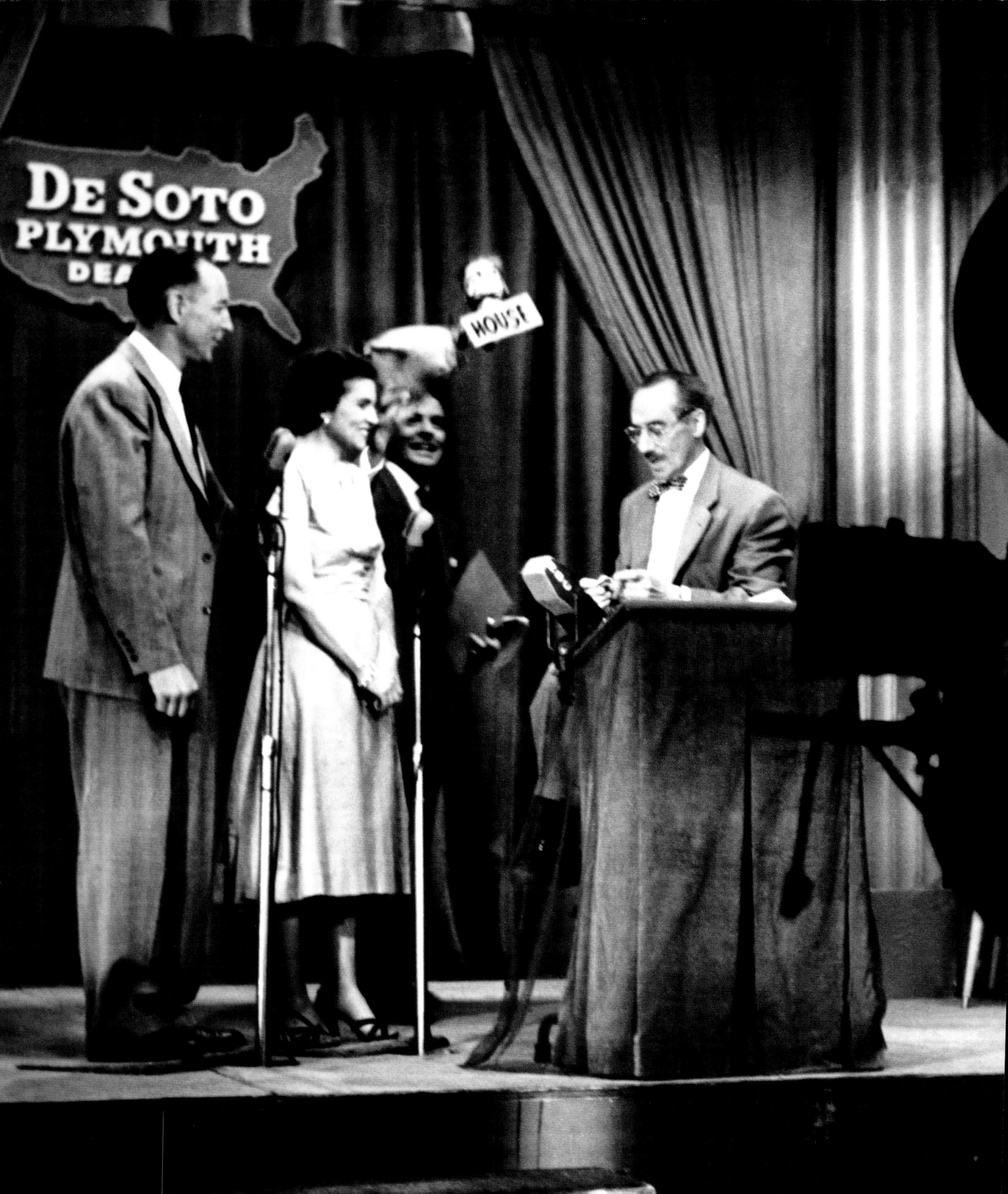
DE SOTO
PLYMOUTH
HOUSE

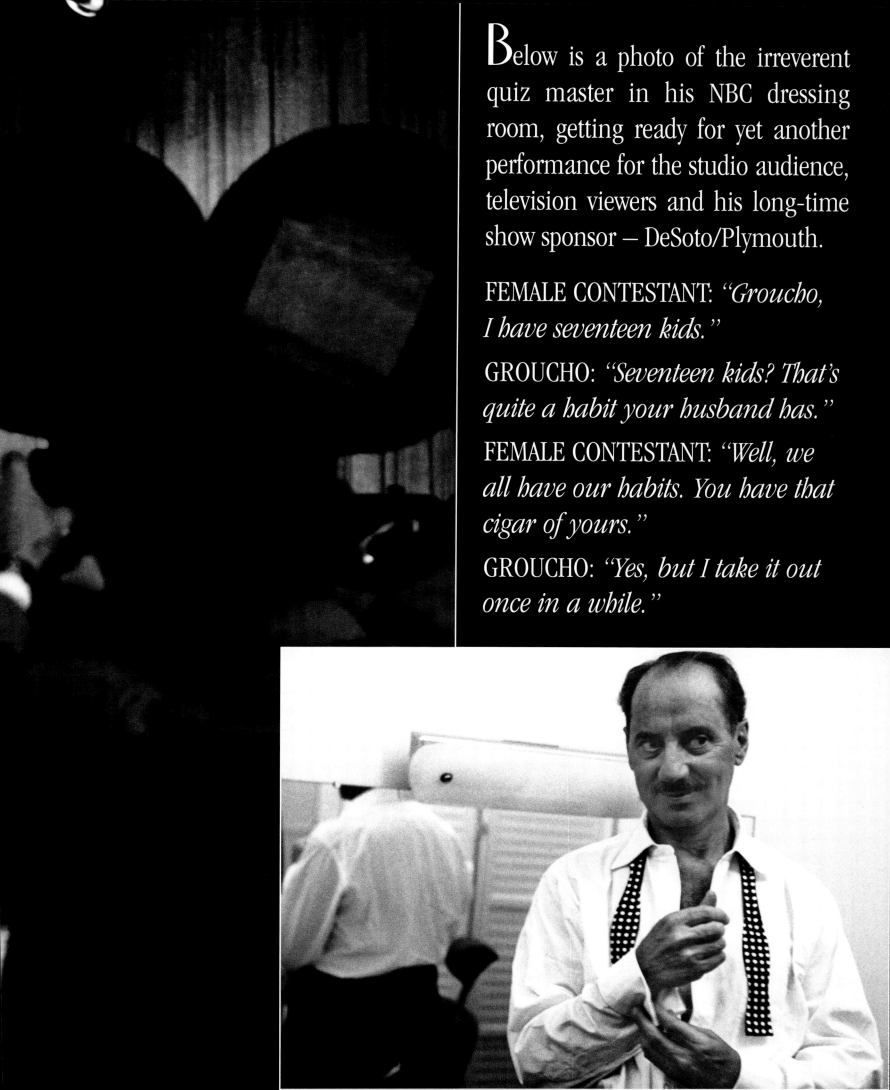

Below is a photo of the irreverent quiz master in his NBC dressing room, getting ready for yet another performance for the studio audience, television viewers and his long-time show sponsor – DeSoto/Plymouth.

FEMALE CONTESTANT: *"Groucho, I have seventeen kids."*

GROUCHO: *"Seventeen kids? That's quite a habit your husband has."*

FEMALE CONTESTANT: *"Well, we all have our habits. You have that cigar of yours."*

GROUCHO: *"Yes, but I take it out once in a while."*

Groucho described the perfect date as someone who looked like Marilyn Monroe, but spoke like George S. Kaufman. Below is a rare candid of Marilyn Monroe on the set of "Love Happy," in which she was 'discovered.' The 1949 film marked the screen return of the Marx Brothers...also, their finish.

The film's cast included Vera-Ellen (above right) and Eric Blore (seated below), with Chico and Father in the role of Sam Grunion, private eye.

MARILYN: *"Two men are following me."*   GROUCHO: *"I can't understand why."*

Frank Sinatra and Jane Russell co-star with Groucho in "Double Dynamite," released in 1951.

On the set, Groucho observed that Sinatra would have made an outstanding film director.

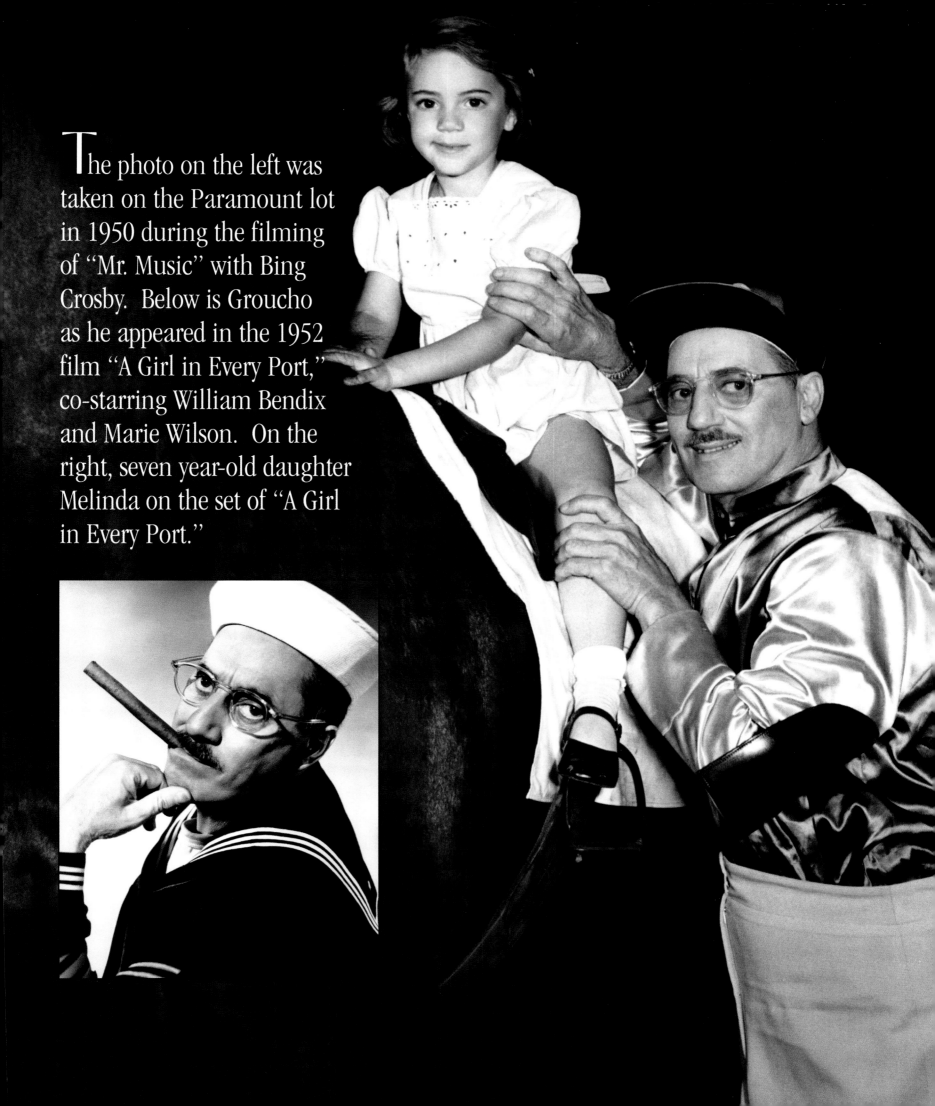

The photo on the left was taken on the Paramount lot in 1950 during the filming of "Mr. Music" with Bing Crosby. Below is Groucho as he appeared in the 1952 film "A Girl in Every Port," co-starring William Bendix and Marie Wilson. On the right, seven year-old daughter Melinda on the set of "A Girl in Every Port."

Groucho as Grand Marshal of the Santa Claus Lane Parade down Hollywood Boulevard in 1953. He is flanked by his daughter Melinda and his grandson, my son Steve.

GROUCHO: *Now, here's the final clause. This is what's known as the sanity clause.*

CHICO: *"Oh, no. You can't fool me. I know there ain't no Sanity Clause."*
— *A Night at the Opera*

'You Bet Your Life'
Starring GROUCHO MARX

Father married a third time in 1954 to Eden Hartford. Groucho was sixty-four, Eden was 24. They divorced in 1968. Here the couple spend several nights out with my half-sister Melinda. The bottom photo shows Groucho and wife Eden on the set of 1957's "The Story of Mankind."

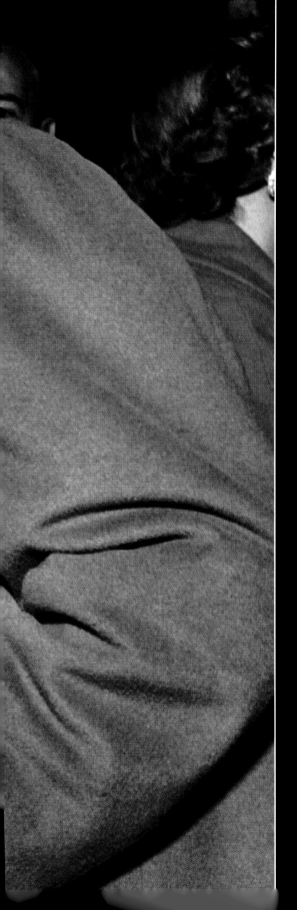

A challenging game of backyard basketball between Father and yours truly in 1954.

Below is a shot I took of my sons Andy Marx, age six, and Steve Marx, age ten, practicing to be studio executives.

On the left, a photo I shot of Groucho practicing to be a father the second time around.

A bevy of beauties hover over comedian Jimmy Durante, Uncle Harpo and my father in the mid-Fifties at an NBC studio. Harpo is wearing a toupee. Dad seems to have left his at home.

My father once referred to Red Skelton as "the logical successor to Chaplin." Here they are at a costume party engaged in a game of dueling cigars.

On the right, Groucho plays a cameo role with Jayne Mansfield in the 1957 film, "Will Success Spoil Rock Hunter."

Below, is a television camera card taken from the show in which Groucho fulfilled a lifetime fantasy – performing as KoKo, the Lord High Executioner in Gilbert & Sullivan's "The Mikado." It was the highest rated NBC special of 1960.

BELL TELEPHONE HOUR
COLOR FRIDAY
NBC

The original photographs are from Groucho's own collection.

Laughing Cavalier

American Gothic

In the summer of 1959, my first wife, Irene, and I took our kids for a seaside vacation at the Hotel del Coronado across the bay from San Diego. When I walked out on the beach the afternoon we arrived, I was surprised to see Oscar-winning director and writer, Billy Wilder, filming a picture starring Marilyn Monroe, Tony Curtis and Jack Lemmon. I had no idea what the picture was, until Wilder, who I knew from the Tennis Club, sat me down on a piece of driftwood between takes and said, "Arthur, this is either going to be the worst picture ever made or one of the greatest. It's about two guys who dress in drag and take refuge in an all-girl band in order to escape from some gangsters they saw commit a massacre in Chicago and who want to rub them out so they can't be witnesses." At the time, the film was still untitled, but it later became known as the classic "Some Like It Hot." Fortunately, I had my camera along, and was able to get a couple of good shots of Monroe in a swimsuit. In the shot on the left, Billy Wilder is seen walking towards my camera with Marilyn and Jack Lemmon (also in the shots below) in the background.

(Below) Marilyn with her arm around my son Steve.

167

Groucho dancing with Audrey Hepburn at one of the rare Hollywood occasions where he agreed to put on a tux. The photos on the right show Audrey and husband Mel Ferrer at the same event, and my father escorting my half-sister Melinda at the Thalian's charity dinner dance in 1959.

In 1963, Robert Fisher and I created, developed and produced "The Mickey Rooney Show" for ABC. It was a funny show, but, unfortunately, we ran on Wednesdays at 9:00 opposite "The Dick Van Dyke Show." In one episode, Mickey gets his foot caught in the car wash chain belt — and winds up getting washed himself. With the schedule we were on, it's possible this was his first bath of the week. I took the shot on location.

(LEFT) Eden, Groucho, Lois and Irwin Allen (who produced "The Poseidon Adventure" and "The Tower-ing Inferno") in a booth at the Brown Derby. Behind them are celebrity caricatures which decorated the walls of the old Hollywood Brown Derby. When Groucho first came to Hollywood, Bob Cobb, owner of the Derby restaurants, sent the restaurant's caricaturist over to his table to do him, so he, too, could be framed and hung on the wall. When the caricaturist finished, he handed his handiwork to Groucho in order for him to autograph it. Iconoclast that he was, Groucho quickly scribbled across his likeness, "To Al Levy's Tavern, the best restaurant on Vine Street." Levy's Tavern was across Vine Street from The Derby and Cobb's biggest competition. Cobb took one look at the inscription and tore up the caricature, which for years caused Derby customers and fans of Groucho to wonder why their favorite comedian's likeness never made the galaxy of stars gracing the famous walls.

On the right: This is my favorite photo of my wife, Lois, taken by me in our favorite city, Paris, in an outdoor café off the Champs-Elysees.

The Groucho Show

NBC flattered Father in 1960 by renaming "You Bet Your Life" as "The Groucho Show." In 1961, after fourteen years, the program's run ended. Father returned to television briefly on CBS in 1962 in a revamped version of "You Bet Your Life" entitled "Tell It to Groucho" — the show from which these publicity photos were taken.

One of the last photos of all five Marx Brothers together in 1957. From left to right they are Gummo, Zeppo, Chico, Groucho and Harpo. Chico, the Italian-accented, piano-playing rogue, died October 11, 1961 at seventy-four. Groucho had a love/hate relationship with Chico. My father was always jealous of Chico's prowess with women and their mother Minnie's preference for Chico. Yet, the brothers spoke everyday. After Chico's funeral, I witnessed my father break his pattern of moderation as the memories caught up with him.

At dinner that night, he proceeded to get drunk on scotch. Harpo's death followed in 1964. He was seventy-five. In a letter to Betty Comden, Groucho wrote, "Having worked with Harpo for forty years, which is longer than most marriages last, his death left quite a void in my life. He was worth all the wonderful adjectives that were used to describe him…" One of the very few times I ever saw my father cry was at Harpo's funeral.

Father started playing golf while he was in vaudeville and, despite having one of the best practice swings in the game, was never able to break ninety. He did, however, make a hole-in-one early in his links career, at the famous Braeburn Country Club outside of Boston. That feat made the sports page of the Boston Globe, with a picture of him between one of Bobby Jones and Frances Ouimet. The caption read, "Groucho Joins the Immortals." The next day a phalanx of reporters and photographers showed up at Braeburn to catch this wizard of the links in action. This time around Groucho took fourteen strokes on the same par three where he'd made the hole-in-one. The next morning there appeared another picture of Groucho between Jones and Ouimet. This time the caption said, "Groucho Leaves the Immortals."

Below, Groucho contemplates another dismal round.

Greeting entertainer Danny
Kaye backstage in Las Vegas
after Kaye's opening in 1964

In 1965, Robert Fisher and I wrote "The Impossible Years." New York reviews were mixed, but it was a play for the audience and ran for 656 sold-out performances on Broadway. Cecil Smith, drama critic for the Los Angeles Times wrote, "This may not be 'Hamlet,' but it's such a funny play that I predict it will be around in stock and amateur productions twenty years from now." He was wrong. I'm still receiving royalties nearly forty years later.

Having my first hit on Broadway was a major thrill, especially after being known as "Groucho's son" all my life. This changed when my father, who wasn't able to attend our opening night at The Playhouse on 48th Street, phoned me several weeks later and said he was going to New York and would I please see that he got the "house seats?" I assured him it was a done deal, and that he wouldn't have to pay for them. But the night he and Eden showed up at the Playhouse box office, and he asked for his tickets, the girl at the ticket window, said, "That'll be fifteen dollars, please." "Fifteen dollars!" he exclaimed in a wounded tone. "I'm getting them for nothing." "Who are you?" she asked. "Don't you know who I am? I'm Arthur Marx's father."

In the photo on the far left, are producer David Black, myself, Alan King and Black's co-producer, Walter Hyman, on opening night, October 13, 1965. That was my first and only tuxedo.

On the left, is a shot of me standing in front of the Forrest Theater in Philadelphia while we were on our try-out tour of "The Impossible Years."

DAVID BLACK and WALTER A. HYMAN

ALAN KING

IMPOSSIBLE YEARS

Comedy by BOB FISHER and ARTHUR MARX

with
JANET WARD
BERT CONVY   SUDIE BOND   MICHAEL VALE
JACK HOLLANDER   NEVA SMALL   MICHAEL HADGE
and
JANE ELLIOT

WILLIAM PITKIN   Lighting by MARTIN ARONSTEIN   Costumes by ANN ROTH

directed by ARTHUR STORCH

FORREST
6 to SEPT. 18
MATINEES WED. & SAT. 2 PM — EVES. 8:30
OPENING NIGHT CURTAIN — 7:30 PM

My son Andy brandishes his grandfather's cigar in my 1968 snapshot on the right. In the photo below is my wife, Lois, Groucho and Gummo. Gummo retired voluntarily from the Marx Brothers' act by the request of the other three brothers and was replaced by their youngest sibling, Zeppo — which was revenge of the worst kind. (Actually, Gummo enlisted during WWI.)

In the bottom photo, taken in 1972, Groucho and Lois clutch Elsie, a poodle pup, which we gave Groucho as a consolation prize to replace Eden after she divorced him.

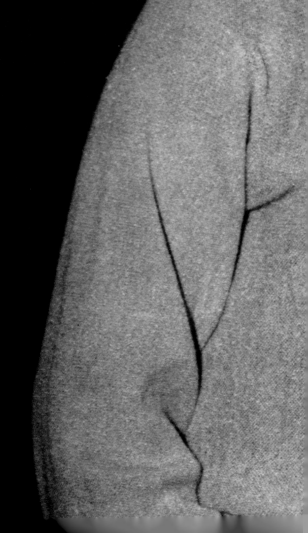

A photograph of Groucho in 1975 at age eighty-five (far left)... still ferocious, cynical and funny.

At the piano, Father practices for his "An Evening With Groucho" concert at Carnegie Hall in 1972.

Every father and son relationship has its ups and downs. Ours included. I must say, Groucho could always make me laugh...as evidenced by my favorite photo of Father and me. He still had it at age eighty-two.

GROUCHO: *"I hope they bury me near a straight man."*

On August 19, 1977, my father shuffled off this mortal coil. He was eighty-six and had battled pneumonia for several months. After he passed away, I kissed his forehead. And contemplated his legacy not as the world's funniest man — but as my father.

"IF YOU KEEP HAVING BIRTHDAYS, YOU'LL EVENTUALLY DIE. LOVE, GROUCHO"

AFTERWORD: The Legacy

In 1985, I received a letter from a student at USC named Frank Ferrante. He wrote that he was doing a one-man show of Groucho song and dance numbers at a charity benefit at USC the following Friday night, and would I be so kind as to come down to one of his rehearsals at the college and give him some pointers? So, I thought, "What the hell? I might as well do something nice for someone for once in my life."

Frank Ferrante as Groucho Marx.

So, I traipsed down to USC on a hot, smoggy day in Spring, and watched Frank Ferrante do his stuff. His physical likeness to Groucho while dressed in his Captain Spaulding outfit was amazing, and the fidelity of his voice and movements while doing all the classic Groucho material from stage and screen knocked me out. He didn't need any help from me, and I told him so. He was as good as the real thing

It turned out that Frank, a theater major, had been a Marx Brothers fan since he was nine years old. He had a roomful of Marx Brothers film posters. He'd been doing Groucho imitations since he was a little boy. He owned a trunkful of Groucho memorabilia. Not only that, he'd seen other actors perform as Groucho, and thought he could do better.

I thought he could, too. But just to prove I wasn't being overly enthusiastic, I brought a number of people down to USC to watch the actual performance. My sister, sons, my wife and Morrie Ryskind, who had co-written with George Kaufman "The Cocoanuts," "Animal Crackers" and "A Night at the Opera," were all in attendance. Ryskind's opinion was more important than anyone's. Frank performed superbly in front of a very, very large audience. Morrie Ryskind was particularly impressed, and so was my sister, Miriam, who usually hated any actor imitating our father.

Before going home that night, I told Frank Ferrante that I wished I had known about him earlier because I just cast my own Groucho show. "However," I assured Frank, "if I ever get another venue where they want my Groucho show, you've got the part." Frank didn't believe me. He thought I was just giving him some Hollywood crap, and that he'd never hear from me again. But I fooled him. A week later, I was contacted by Richard Carrothers, who owned Tiffany's Attic Dinner Theater in Kansas City, Missouri. He wanted to have a Groucho show in his theater. I told him I knew a young man who was the best Groucho. "Unfortunately," I added, "he isn't a big name. In fact he's no name at all. Just a student finishing up at USC." Surprisingly, for most producers aren't like this, Carrothers replied, "I don't care if he's unknown, just as long as he's good." "Then you have a deal," I told him.

Although I'd been impressed with Frank as the young Groucho, I still wasn't sure if he could handle the scenes of Groucho as an old man, which was an important part of the show. So, before I committed myself to Frank, I invited him to my collaborator's house the next day to have him read the "old man" scene for us. My collaborator, Bob Fisher, and I were standing in his living room, looking out his picture window onto Alpine Drive, eagerly awaiting Frank's arrival, when a car pulled up to the curb. An old man in a beret, white turtleneck sweater and navy blue jacket with a lit cigar shuffled slowly up the walk to the front door.

Frank's impersonation of Groucho at age eighty-five, the shaky old man's voice he used when he greeted us, was so realistic that at first glance I thought my father had been resurrected from the grave, and I wasn't too sure I was happy about that. "Hello, Big Feet," the old man wheezed. I was relieved, however, when I realized it was only Frank, playing the part. Frank only had to read a few lines in the "old man" scene to convince Bob and me that we had finally found the perfect Groucho Marx for Kansas City. Now, we had the ingredient for a promising comedy for Broadway. The Kansas City critics thought so, too, and we sold out for eight weeks.

That was enough to convince Richard Carrothers and his partner Dennis Hennessey to take "Groucho: A Life in Revue" to New York. After some rough moments during six weeks of rehearsals, we managed to make the show as good as it had been in Kansas City. Nevertheless, we weren't sure if that was good enough to please New York.

The following October 8th, 1986 we opened at New York's Lucille Lortel Theatre in the Village. The show and Frank received rave reviews from every New York critic. We played a year with both the show and Frank receiving a number of off-Broadway awards and the following year, we opened at the Comedy Theatre in London's West End, with similar kudos from the British critics. We were also nominated for the Laurence Olivier Award for 'Best Comedy Production' of the 1987 season.

And I'm equally happy to report that Frank and I are still the best of friends, despite having been through the war of putting a successful show on in New York.

Frank Ferrante and Arthur Marx attend the New York opening night party of "Groucho: A Life in Revue" on October 8th, 1986.

- ARTHUR MARX

ACKNOWLEDGEMENTS

Every square inch of this book is influenced by the design of Jerry Eggers.
Thank you, Jerry, for your talent and for treating the Marx Family with great respect through your artistry.

Thanks to Ralph Torres who spearheaded this project and contributed his keen eye, enormous talent, energy and skill as photography editor.

Gratitude must go to Cindy and Dave Casey of Phoenix Marketing Services, Inc. without whom this book simply would not exist.

And to those loving friends and supporters who helped lead the way:
Jeff Petredes; Bernard Havard; Peter LeDonne; Alan Foster; Alison White; The Public Broadcasting System;
Dave Bynum, Richard Carrothers; Dennis Hennessey; Jody Kielbasa; Jim Williamson; Cathy Kosley; The Ferrante Families;
The Torres Families; Toper Taylor; Christie Dreyfuss; Irene Weibel; Nelvana Communications, Inc.;
Dawn Perez; Debbie Marquez; Virginia Austin Curtis; Prof. William C. White; Sr. Rachel; Kelly and Christina Porter;
Paul Wesolowski; Roy Abramsohn; Marguerite Lowell; Paul Stavros; The Berriz Family; Mark Sylvester; James B. McKenzie;
Mark Jansky; David and June Rogers; Mike Beauregard; Karen Schmidt; The University of Southern California-Division of Drama;
St. Rita's Church; Br. Donald Mansir; Br. Malachy Biller; La Salle High School (Pasadena); Jim Furmston;
Brad Selsor; Jim Grady; Lily and Brandy; Amanda Rogers; James Goble; The Hoertig Family, Steve Marx and Lois Marx.

FOR INFORMATION REGARDING THE MARX BROTHERS MAGAZINE,
"THE FREEDONIA GAZETTE,"
CONTACT PAUL WESOLOWSKI AT
335 FIELDSTONE DRIVE, NEW HOPE, PA 18938-1012
or E-MAIL AT tfg@cheerful.com

Visit our website at www.grouchoworld.com

PHOTO CREDITS

ARTHUR MARX, PHOTOGRAPHER
Pages: iii, 51-57, 59-67, 68 (right), 69-77, 79-81, 86-89, 100, 101, 103,
105-111, 114, 115, 156, 157 (lower right), 166, 167, 170, 171, 176, 179, 180, 181.

ARTHUR MARX COLLECTION
Pages: v, 1-16, 19, 22, 24, 25, 29, 32, 36, 37, 40-43, 50, 58, 68 (left), 78, 83, 91,
98, 99, 102, 104, 131-136, 141-143, 145, 151 (left), 152, 153, 157 (upper left),
158, 159, 162-165, 168, 169 (lower right), 178, 182-185, 190.

PAUL WESOLOWSKI COLLECTION
Pages: 17, 18, 20, 21, 23, 26-28, 30, 31, 33-35, 38, 39, 44-49, 82, 84, 85, 90, 92-97,
112, 113, 116-130, 137-140, 144, 146-150, 151 (right), 154, 155, 160, 161,
169 (upper right), 172-175, 177.

Thanks to the following photographers:
Pages:
i. Ralph Torres;
ii. Theresa Ferrante;
iv, 190. Michael Levee, Jr.;
116-130, 144, 157 (upper right). Gene Lester;
143. Bill Helms;
179. Lois Marx;
182. Sam Perrin;
186. Courtesy Arkansas Repertory Theatre;
187. Adam Newman.

And gratitude to the following:
The American Broadcasting Company, the Columbia Broadcasting System,
the National Broadcasting Company, Metro-Goldwyn-Mayer, Inc.,
RKO Radio Pictures, United Artists, Universal Pictures and
Bell Telephone Company.

Cover montage photos from the collections of Arthur Marx and Paul Wesolowski.

Back jacket: Photos by Ken Hively, Los Angeles Times.

Back flap: Photos by Patrick Vingo.

Dust jacket design by Jerry Eggers.

Arthur Marx, as a teenager, shoots a sunset at Coronado, California.